LIVING IN GOSHEN

The Goshen Chronicles

Elijah Centre
**Project
Heritage**

The Goshen Chronicles

Based on the "Living in Goshen" Series
Created by Elijah Centre Project Heritage

Orginally printed in Trinidad & Tobago
First Printing 2020

ISBN 978-976-43-0019-9

**Congress
PublishingHouse**

Dedicated to the Children of Congress WBN

Keep Goshen in your hearts!

Table of Contents

The Plague of Blood

A long time ago when Moses walked the land,
God told him,
"Take your brother Aaron, with his staff in his hand.
Go to the ruler over Egypt, the one they call Pharaoh.
Tell him, I command him,
'Let the Israelites go!' "

They did exactly as God said, Moses and Aaron.
They told Pharaoh what God had said, but he would not listen.
So God commanded Moses,
"Strike the water with that rod!"

Then all the water in Egypt turned into blood.

The Plague of Frogs

Remember Pharaoh?

He disobeyed God's command.
And water turned to blood all across the land.

Seven days later, God told Moses:
"Go back to Pharaoh,
Tell him again I said, 'Let the Israelites go!' "

But Pharaoh would not listen to Moses or to God.

So the entire land was covered by a plague of frogs.

The Plague of Lice

Pharaoh summoned Moses.
"Moses, pray to the Lord!
Take away these frogs from Egypt," Pharaoh
implored.

Moses prayed; the frogs died, and were
gathered in a pile.
The only frogs left were those living in the Nile.

The Egyptians were relieved but Pharaoh's
heart was full of meanness;
Moses had kept his word but Pharaoh did not
keep his promise -
to set the Israelites free to offer God their
sacrifice.
So God told Aaron, **"Strike the ground!" and
the ground turned to lice!**

Operation
Egypt
ROSETTA
ALEXANDRIA
TANIS
GOSHEN
LOWER
EGYPT
CAIRO
MEMPHIS
HERMOPOLIS
BADARI
Nile
Red Sea
NAQADA
THEBES
Empire of Egypt
UPPER
EGYPT
ASWAN

The Plague of Flies

The Lord then said to Moses,
"Tomorrow, as Pharaoh heads to the river,
Confront him along the way and this message
you must deliver:

'The Lord says: Free my people so that they
may worship me
Or I will send a plague of flies, the worst you'll
ever see!
Swarms of flies will cover Egypt by this time
tomorrow,
Every Egyptian will be afflicted, even you the
Pharaoh.
But I will make a distinction between your
people and mine;

There will be no flies in Goshen!
Take this as a sign!'"

The Plague on Livestock

Once again Pharaoh summoned Moses to his
great big palace:
"Pray away these flies and I'll free the
Israelites—I promise!"

But Moses did not trust Pharaoh who had
deceived him in the past.
He knew that once the flies were gone,
Pharaoh's promise would not last.

Still, Moses prayed to the Lord and the flies did
indeed depart.
But Pharaoh would not free God's people,
instead he hardened his heart.
So God sent Pharaoh a warning; this is what
He said:
"Free my people or all Egyptian livestock
will drop dead!"

The Plague of Boils

As Pharaoh hardened his heart, God continued with His plans;
He sent yet another plague upon the Egyptians.

He told Moses and Aaron, "From a furnace, take the ashes
And toss them into the air while Pharaoh watches.

The ashes will turn to fine dust over all of Egypt;
Every person, every animal will be stricken, NONE shall be skipped.

When Moses throws the ashes up into the air,
Painful boils on all Egyptians will suddenly appear."

The Plague of Hail

Then the Lord said to Moses,
"Get up early in the morning,
Confront hard-hearted Pharaoh and issue him
this warning:

'Free my people now, that's what I, the Lord,
command
Or I'll send the full force of my plagues against
you and your land!

Tell your people take their animals and lock
themselves inside.
I am the Lord almighty, my power won't be
denied.
I will send the worst hailstorm Egypt has ever
known,
By this time tomorrow and MY power
WILL be known!' "

The Plague of Locusts

Only in Goshen did peace and safety prevail;
No Israelite or his property had been destroyed
by hail.

Pharaoh cried out for mercy-said he'd let the
Israelites go.
But when God stopped the hail, his answer was
still, "No!"

The Lord sent Moses back to Pharaoh as He'd
done from the start,
But Pharaoh-oh so stubborn! -refused to
humble his heart.

He would not free God's people; he enjoyed
being mean.
**So God sent a plague of locusts that ate the
land clean!**

The Plague of Darkness

Pharaoh summoned Moses and Aaron once more.
He asked them to pray away this plague, like they'd done before.

Moses prayed and the Lord sent a wind that blew strongly –
All the locusts were swept away into the Red Sea.

Pharaoh continued to ignore the Lord's command.
So God commanded Moses, "Stretch out your hand!

Let darkness cover Egypt and hide everything in sight,
Only in Goshen will there be light!"

The Plague on the Firstborn

When the darkness lifted, Pharaoh was still
unkind.
He told Moses, "Take your people, but your
livestock stays behind."

Moses declined that offer even though it
sounded nice.
He said, "We need our livestock too, to offer
God our sacrifice."

Pharaoh grew angry and reacted in spite.
He shouted at Moses, "Get out of my sight!"

The Lord saw how Pharaoh treated Moses with
scorn
And sent a plague of death upon Egyptian first-
born.

The Exodus

The plague of death was terrible, even Pharaoh
had lost his son.
He knew he'd been defeated and the God of
Moses had won.

Pharaoh could fight no more, he summoned
Moses and said: "Please,
Take every Israelite, what they own, and leave!"

The obedient Israelites followed Moses' next instructions.

They took silver, gold and clothing from neighbouring Egyptians.

But when Pharaoh heard that the Israelites had fled -
He changed his mind about their freedom and chased after them instead!

The Lord's Declaration

Don't cry out to me Moses,
Raise your staff, stretch out your hand.
The waters of the sea will part;
and there will be dry land.

The evil Egyptians will give chase across
the dry ground.
Every Israelite will be saved;
every Egyptian will be drowned.

I am the Lord, and all Egyptians will soon
know
The glory of the Lord when I destroy their
Pharaoh!

The Lord's Victory

Moses raised his staff
and stretched it towards the Red Sea.
The walls of water rushed back in their
place - covering Pharaoah's entire army.

The Israelite's rejoiced.
God had finally set them free!
And from that day each one of them
remembered
How the Lord had the final victory.

"Living in Goshen" was produced by Elijah Centre Project Heritage.

Elijah Centre is a unique, global, borderless, Kingdom community, founded on biblical principles and recognizing Jesus Christ as its head. With its primary base in Trinidad & Tobago, called the Nexus, Elijah Centre has locations in cities around the globe, referred to as Embassies. For more information, visit:

www.elijahcentre.org

Project Heritage is the People Group ministry within Elijah Centre for children up to age 11. Project Heritage focuses on holistic development based on the pattern of maturity demonstrated by Jesus throughout his childhood. For more information, visit:

www.projectheritage.org

Elijah Centre is the Creative Core of Congress WBN, a global, faith-based organization affecting human, social and national transformation throughout the earth. For more information, visit:

www.congresswbn.org

www.ingramcontent.com/pod-product-compliance
Lightning Source LLC
Chambersburg PA
CBHW040902110726
48005CB00001B/165